Spotlight on Reading

Story Elements

Grades 5–6

Carson-Dellosa Publishing LLC
Greensboro, North Carolina

Credits

Layout and Cover Design: Van Harris

Development House: The Research Masters

Cover Photo: Image Copyright Darrin Henry, 2011 Used under license from Shutterstock.com

Visit *carsondellosa.com* for correlations to Common Core, state, national, and Canadian provincial standards.

Carson-Dellosa Publishing, LLC
PO Box 35665
Greensboro, NC 27425 USA
www.carsondellosa.com

ISBN 978-16-099-6494-8
08-116217784

About the Book

In this book, the elements necessary to critique and discuss a story are reviewed. Teachers, parents, and students who read through the pages of this workbook are encouraged to consider such literary elements as genre, character, setting, action, plot, subplot, climax, point of view, and conflict/problem.

Pages from this book can be used individually to strengthen the recognition of a specific element, or to introduce it as a topic. Workbook activities can also act as springboards prior to creative writing sessions. Teachers might want to use certain pages on more difficult concepts—such as point of view—to help review the material after it has been worked on in class.

• •

Table of Contents

Name _____

"Write" Now

Circle the correct genre to complete each sentence. Then write the genre next to each title on the list below.

• •

1. A story set on another planet would probably be _____ .

    science fiction   biography   historical fiction

2. A book of haiku written in the fifteenth century would be _____ .

    drama   poetry   adventure

3. A book set in New Orleans during the American Civil War most likely would be _____ .

    fairy tale   fantasy   historical fiction

4. A book about the life of Martin Luther King Jr. would be a _____ .

    poetry   biography   mystery

5. A book with talking animals as characters probably would be a _____ .

    biography   mystery   folktale

6. Cinderella _____

7. Middle School on Mars _____

8. The Life of Sitting Bull _____

9. The Knight and the Dragon _____

10. Rhymes for All Seasons _____

Story Elements • CD-104558

Name _____

Different Kinds of Stories

Read each paragraph. Circle the correct genre.

• •

1. I hopped on the magnet-van after my
group meeting at the Edu-plex. We had met
to discuss research for our paper, entitled
"Foods Across the Galaxies." We could have
met by hologram, but our mentor, Sean
Wang, suggested that we share the same space. So now I am riding in this
magnet-van, zipping along 20 feet above the flat surface of the Gobi Desert.

   fantasy   realistic fiction   historical fiction   science fiction

2. Grandpa held me in his arms as he stretched his wings. Lifting up into the
air, he flew us over the forest. "It's OK, Petey. I won't let go." I just had to
cry, so I pressed my face into Grandpa's shoulder and wept softly. We
were moving to a new forest and I hated to leave my old home behind.
I could tell we were slowing down and dropping steadily. "Almost there,"
murmured Grandpa. We landed in front of our clan's new tree home.
Grandpa folded his wings and we went inside.

   fantasy   realistic fiction   historical fiction   science fiction

3. Pa handed me the lantern. "C'mon, Jesse," he mumbled. "The fence is
broken and we've got to fix it before any cows get loose." I hurried after
him, realizing we did not have time to waste. Last year, we lost several
calves and it really hurt us. Most of the ranch hands had gone into town
to unwind before next week's trail ride. So, Pa only had me for help. After
he grabbed his tools, we stepped into the night air and headed for the
eastern side of the fence.

   fantasy   realistic fiction   historical fiction   science fiction

4. I want nothing to do with the flower store! Mom's business was good for her
. . . and good for our whole family. But, I want to work at the art gallery. Mrs.
Fleming suggested that I assist her at the gallery with her Saturday morning
class. Those small children are so much fun to teach. But, Mom wants me to
help her on the weekends, and I do not know what to do.

   fantasy   realistic fiction   historical fiction   science fiction

What Is It?

Read the paragraphs. Choose a genre from the Word Bank. Write it on the line below each paragraph.

• •

Word Bank

| biography | myth | tall tale | realistic fiction | science fiction |

1. When Daniel Boone was a small child, he came down with smallpox. According to one story, he got tired of playing outside when all his friends were sick in bed. So, he snuck into bed with them. A few days later, Daniel got the pox. His mother was angry—and scared.

   _____

2. Why, our winters got so cold the lakes would freeze in minutes. That is how Lost Lake vanished. You see, a large—or rather, gigantic—flock of geese settled down upon it and their feet froze in the water in short order. When they flew off the following morning, they took the whole lake with them.

   _____

3. Ida looked at the girl who stood in the doorway. She was Ida's clone! It was like looking into a mirror. There was no difference in face, form, coloring, even stance. That Doctor Enselmeier! He must have perfected his clone creation project.

   _____

4. All three boys spun out on their bikes, gravel flying. School was out! Ted, in the lead as always, headed toward the park. Pumping hard, the boys sped up Hollow Hill, through the sandlot, and across the ballpark, slamming on their brakes just shy of the bleachers.

   _____

5. "Whatever you do, do not open the box, my dear." But Pandora marveled at the box before her. It was so beautiful, what could possibly be inside? The temptation was too great to resist. Pandora was such a curious girl that she could not help but to lift the lid for a quick peek. But when she did, dark spirits suddenly flew out. They took the skies and spread all over the world. What had she done?

   _____

6. By the time Zach was five, he had grown to six feet, eight inches. His appetite was so great that his dad worked twelve hours a day just to provide Zach's meals. His voice had deepened, though he still carried a blanket and sucked his thumb. The blanket he adored was a twenty-pound quilt that his father made for him from a 200-pound pile of old clothes.

   _____

Name _____

Who Is It?

First, match the name of each character with the most likely description.
Then, create names for the group of people on the list below.

• •

_____ 1. Leo Lyons

_____ 2. Melodie Singer

_____ 3. Spuds Brown

_____ 4. Macon Potts

_____ 5. Lollie Popp

_____ 6. Ripp Kord

_____ 7. Tex Ryder

_____ 8. Stretch VanderHoop

_____ 9. Minnie Follows

_____ 10. Grace Whirling

_____ 11. Auntie Pasta

_____ 12. Willie Tripp

a. a ceramic-loving artist who sculpts pottery

b. a potato farmer from north-central Idaho

c. a four-year-old girl with sticky hands

d. a music teacher who instructs young singers

e. a stunt man known for his parachute jumps

f. a zoologist who studies African lions

g. an accident-prone boy who constantly slips and falls

h. a seven-foot tall basketball star

i. a horse-loving cowhand who spends his days in the saddle

j. a petite young girl who loves to tag along with others

k. a ballerina known for her elegant pirouettes

l. an older woman who loves to cook spaghetti

13. a librarian _____

14. a train engineer _____

15. a senator _____

16. a firefighter _____

17. a golf pro _____

18. a scientist _____

Stretching It

Read the sentences. They describe details from different stories. If the detail best fits a realistic story, write an **R** on the line. If the detail best fits a fantasy story, write an **F** on the line.

• •

_____ 1. My dog, Petey, loves to eat ham sandwiches. He tries to swipe mine every chance he gets.

_____ 2. Lana's feet were sore. Walking two miles through the museum in one afternoon had worn holes in her sneakers.

_____ 3. Seth enjoyed hanging out with his friend, Ibit. He wished he could spend more time at Ibit's house, but he was allergic to the atmosphere on Jupiter.

_____ 4. Ping could not wait until the new television arrived. He was excited about having a 3-D screen in his very own home.

_____ 5. Haley was in tears. She had lost her ticket to the concert, and the show was sold out!

_____ 6. Will was frustrated with his soccer team. They did not play as well after robots joined the team.

_____ 7. Scamper is the best pet in the world! She fetches and comes when I call her. The only problem is feeding her. It costs a lot to feed a dinosaur.

_____ 8. Quinn had a hard time walking barefoot across the hot sandy beach. As soon as she could, she dived into the water to cool off.

_____ 9. Irina made an incredible sculpture out of ice. She was sure that it would win the top prize at the arts festival.

_____ 10. Luka loved sitting in the hot tub. On a clear night, he could see one or two spaceships cross the sky.

Name _____

Read lines of dialogue from different stories. Match each quote with the correct character from the list.

• •

Character List
a. Lance Perry, an actor
b. Sharmain Steele, a registered nurse
c. Felix Brecht, a music composer
d. Bitsy Floss, a patriotic seamstress
e. Lee Deezine, a toy designer
f. Goldie Grahame, a nutritionist
g. Bill Gelbrefe, a lawyer
h. Belem El Sher, a carpet exporter
i. Robbie Hollingsworth, a teacher
j. "Lead Foot" LaRue, a truck driver

_____ 1. "Shall I administer another IV? The patient just woke up."

_____ 2. "Well, I enjoy creating toys that are fun for kids. Take this Clyde the Cat wind-up toy, for instance. It always lands on its feet. See?"

_____ 3. "Your daughter is a delight in my classroom. She is always the first one to raise her hand."

_____ 4. "How's my hair? Are you ready to shoot? No, I don't need a stunt man for this scene!"

_____ 5. "A healthy diet should have whole grains and lots of fresh fruits and vegetables."

_____ 6. "Hello, Jacques! Your Persian rugs are ready for shipment. I think you will be delighted when they arrive."

_____ 7. "I have almost finished sewing the flag. I am so excited for everyone to see my stars and stripes design."

_____ 8. "This traffic is making me crazy! It's slowing me down, and this delivery is late!"

_____ 9. "First, the flutes begin the melody. Then, the violins come in."

_____ 10. "Can you repeat that last statement, please? I want to make sure that everyone in the courtroom heard your testimony."

Name _____

The Lair of the Cave Dragon

Read the story. Complete the activity on page 11 by placing an **X** next to the correct answer.

• •

Knight Lazar urged his horse on through the dense woods. He had been riding for hours and the poor animal was breathing hard, but they were very close to the castle. A soldier in gleaming armor met him at the edge of the forest and escorted him through the castle gates.

Entering the throne room, they stood before the king. The soldier announced, "Knight Lazar has arrived, your Majesty." He backed away, leaving the king and knight alone. The king rose from his throne, and filled two silver goblets with water. Handing one to the knight, he kept the other for himself. "What is the challenge, sire?" Knight Lazar asked.

"The cave dragon emerged from her lair three nights ago. She soared into the night, grabbed hold of the moon with her talons, and snatched it from the sky. No one has seen the moon since, and it has created chaos. Someone has to find the moon and bring it back."

"That is a difficult problem, but I am up to the task, your Majesty," replied the knight.

"Wonderful," said the king. "You must leave at once, while it is still light outside because the dragon sleeps during the day."

Knight Lazar quickly gulped down the water in his silver goblet, then he asked the king, "Do you mind if I take this goblet with me?"

"By all means," the king replied. "Although, I cannot see how it could possibly help."

"You will, your Majesty. You will."

Knight Lazar quickly rode to Dragon Mountain. The knight could hear the snores of the sleeping dragon rumbling from the cave's entrance.

He took the silver goblet from his satchel and dipped it into a stream at the bottom of the mountain. The cool water seemed to glisten in the silver goblet. As Knight Lazar glanced down into it, he was sure that his plan would work. He began to climb toward the dragon's lair, making sure not to spill any water.

As he reached the entrance to the cave, he carefully stepped inside. The dragon slept against a cave wall at the back, with her scaly legs wrapped around the moon. The creature had a tight grip on the moon, which shone brightly in the dark cave. It would be impossible for Knight Lazar to pry it free without waking the dragon, but he did not intend to try.

The Lair of the Cave Dragon (cont.)

With the goblet of water in his hand, he walked softly, careful not to wake the sleeping dragon. As he reached the back of the cave, he held the goblet out.

A reflection of the moon appeared in the glistening stream water. It seemed to fill the goblet, which suddenly felt much heavier in Knight Lazar's grasp. He tightened his grip and silently backed away.

Reaching the cave entrance, he spied the sun drooping in the sky. It was dusk and night would be falling very soon. Knight Lazar did not have much time to waste.

At the bottom of the mountain, Knight Lazar stumbled and nearly fell. But he quickly recovered, still holding the goblet. Suddenly, a ball of fire flared from the entrance of the cave. The dragon must have woken up and caught his scent. She knew someone had come into her lair.

Knight Lazar quickly clambered onto his horse. Riding for the forest, he could hear the dragon's giant flapping wings. The creature had left the cave and was in pursuit.

The sky had turned from dusky orange to deep purple. Night had fallen; now was the time. He threw the water from the goblet up into the air, and the moon's reflection sailed into the sky. As the dragon watched the reflection sail over her head, she uttered a shrill cry.

A deep rumble could be heard from the cave. Suddenly, the moon shot out and chased its reflection into the sky. It soared higher and higher, until it was too far up for the dragon to reach. With a sigh, she turned and flew back to her lair. Knight Lazar had saved the day and the night.

1. Who is the hero of this story?
   - _____ a. the king
   - _____ b. the soldier
   - _____ c. the knight

3. What is the setting of this story?
   - _____ a. in a make-believe kingdom
   - _____ b. on the shore of a beach
   - _____ c. on the moon

2. What problem does the hero need to solve?
   - _____ a. He must return the moon to the sky.
   - _____ b. He must locate Dragon Mountain.
   - _____ c. He must search for a magical stream.

4. What is the genre of this story?
   - _____ a. mystery
   - _____ b. fantasy
   - _____ c. contemporary

Name _____

Welcome to Our Assembly

Read lines of dialogue from a story about a school assembly. Match each quote with the correct character from the list.

• •

Character List

a. Tony Brown: very nervous
b. Abby McMann: observant
c. Percy Pennyfeather: nosy; a busybody
d. Nadia Kovacs: arrogant; smug
e. Jodhi Amani: relieved
f. Jamal Davis: disappointed
g. Mary Marshall: serious; in charge
h. Chang Lee: hopeful; talented

_____ 1. "Quiet down, students! We have something important to discuss. I need your attention."

_____ 2. "Oh, no! Do you think they are going to announce our grades?"

_____ 3. "They are probably going to give a major award to the best student, and who else could it be but me!"

_____ 4. "I saw some teachers talking in the hall, but I couldn't overhear them."

_____ 5. "I think this is about that science award. I think I could win. My project turned out well."

_____ 6. "Look! There's that new teacher. I bet this assembly is to welcome her."

_____ 7. "Whew! I was worried they were going to cancel the school-wide festival."

_____ 8. "I thought my friend Chang was going to get that award today. Too bad!"

Name _____

Theme Park

Read the story. Answer each question.

• •

   "That is 17 dollars," announced Cal. He gathered all of the change spread out on his bed and placed it next to the dollar bills on the red comforter. Then, he flopped back onto the bed, making the change bounce.

   "We still need 23 dollars to cover the cost of admission," frowned Cleo. "Mom said we have to have the total cost of admission before we can go to Great Mountain Theme Park." The twins sat on the bed in Cal's room, imagining the theme park. It was sure to have delicious food, great arcade games, and the best rides in the state—roller coasters, water rides, and Ferris wheels.

   "It will take at least a month of allowances to have enough money," said Cal. "Besides, that would not leave any money for food or souvenirs."

   "I know," Cleo said, "and I have already checked between the couch cushions, under the car seats, and in all of our jacket pockets." As the twins sat glumly, they watched colorful leaves drop from the tree outside the window.

   Suddenly, an idea popped into their heads. They could rake the neighbors' leaves for cash. It was the perfect plan. Their mother would be pleased that they helped out the neighborhood, and they would get to go to the amusement park.

   The twins hurried outside, grabbed two rakes from the garage and got to work. By the end of the day, they had all the money they needed. That night, they went to sleep with dreams of the Great Mountain Theme Park floating in their heads.

1. What is the setting?

   _____

2. Who are the characters?

   _____

3. What is the problem?

   _____

4. How do they solve their problem?

   _____

Name _____

I Have a Feeling

Read plot events from different stories. Write the name of a character to answer each question.

· ·

a. Faster than he had ever run before, Lonnie Lorenzo sped through the trees of the city park. None of the other students could catch him. Today, he was in a league of his own and was sure to win the race.

b. She swept into the brightly lit hall. This was her day! Lady Beatrice had ordered all of her lords to come to court and compete for the Golden Scepter. They had better obey!

c. Dorothy Wells stepped onto her porch and scowled at the carload of noisy, rude men parked in front of her house. She was determined to make them move before they woke the rest of the neighborhood.

d. She looked out, shivering with fear. Frank the fox had followed her to her nest. Dora, the young deer mouse, nervously pulled back into the shadows.

e. Boy, did his toe hurt! Steven hobbled over to a chair to look at his big toe. He had pretended to kick his friend Jeremy. Instead, he had kicked the wall. Steven winced as he pulled off his sock.

f. Ned Tuttle climbed into the back seat filled with excitement. Today, he was finally going to have those braces taken off of his teeth!

g. Helene stared at the diving board. It was so far above the swimming pool. Thirty years ago, when she was still a young woman, she could have easily made that dive. But now, she was not so sure. A lot of time had passed. Could she still do it?

   1.   Who is excited about the future? _____

   2.   Who seems ready for a confrontation? _____

   3.   Who feels good about his ability? _____

   4.   Who is thinking about the past? _____

   5.   Who seems nervous and afraid? _____

   6.   Who appears arrogant and determined? _____

   7.   Who is sorry for a mistake? _____

Name _____

Match each line of dialogue with the correct time and place. Then, write a setting for the five quotes on the list below. Be sure to describe both the time and the place.

• •

_____ 1. "Not much happening here. Wonder if the other side of the island is any busier."

_____ 2. "Are those animals stomping over my head? It's enough to give me a headache!"

_____ 3. "Who told Tommy to buy me a lava lamp? What a crazy gift!"

_____ 4. "Whoa! All of this swaying is making me seasick."

_____ 5. "I just wanted to grab a coconut, but now I can't get down!"

a. on a treetop during a summer windstorm

b. on the shore of an island off the coast of Greenland in late autumn

c. up in a palm tree on a summer day

d. under a bridge that three goats try to cross.

e. in the return line at a department store one afternoon

6. "I know it's a kooky style, but I think my hair looks . . . special."

_____

_____

7. "Hey, glad you finally made it to the party. Did you bring your swimsuit?"

_____

_____

8. "Ouch! What just stung me? That hurts."

_____

_____

9. "They're coming this way. Yes, I see them now. What wild costumes!"

_____

_____

10. "Honey, you shouldn't have! It's so expensive, but sure is beautiful."

_____

_____

Name _____

Summer Camp

Read the story. Complete the activity on page 17.

● ●

   Our camp is great. A bunch of kids from school go there, but I especially enjoy meeting new kids from the other schools. We sing crazy songs in the dining hall each day at noon, and there are activities and challenges to complete all day long.

   This year, I got Keesha for a counselor. She is so funny! She has all of us girls rolling on the cabin floor laughing at her funny, silly stories at bedtime. But, she is smart too and knows when one of us is homesick or feeling bad. She never pokes fun of us when we do something stupid, and she shows us how to express kindness to the others in our cabin.

   Keesha loves nature and is studying biology at the university during the school year. She often points out the wildlife in camp. On our second day at camp, Keesha took us on the first of many walks through the woods. At one point, she stopped and pointed to the crook of a beech tree. We saw a mother opossum with four babies on her back. They were so cute!

   Once, Keesha took all ten of us for a hike through the woods at night. She warned us to be quiet and to bring our flashlights with us. We walked for maybe twenty minutes when we stopped suddenly. We heard some chattering creatures off to our right. Down by the lake were two raccoons fighting over some bread they had found. They almost sounded like two children squabbling over a treat.

   One drizzly day, she took us to a nearby national park. We took binoculars, guidebooks, insect repellent, water, and snacks. We sketched some of the wonderful flowering plants we saw. Keesha knew the history and medicinal value of many of these plants. She showed us one plant that gave off a very powerful smell when she broke it open. She told us it would keep flies and mosquitoes away. It was easy to see why that would work because that odor was horrible!

© Carson-Dellosa

16

Story Elements • CD-104558

Summer Camp (cont.)

Every evening after supper we would play games with campers from the other cabins. Keesha volunteered to have our cabin set up the evening game on our fifth day. We walked all over the camp, setting up clues for a treasure hunt, which meant that we had to canoe to different landmarks around the lake, crawl under some of the older cabins, plan hiding spots, and race down the camp trails.

Of course, we ran out of time. When the bell rang for supper, we were still far across the field. My new friend, Rita, unknowingly stepped over a light blue-gray snake. It was huge! Keesha said it was called a blue racer. We all stood back and watched it, talking quietly. "Look how long it is," said Keesha. "It must be as long as I am!" We watched as the startled snake started to move slowly past us, and then suddenly raced away. We were late for supper that day, but it did not matter because we all had such a great time.

I want to go back to camp next summer and learn as much about nature as Keesha knows. That would be amazing!

1. List the two main elements of the setting.
   Time: _____   Place: _____

2. Match each event from the story to the correct time and place. Draw lines to connect them.

EVENT	PLACE	TIME
see baby possums	in field	every noon
sing songs	in crook of the beech tree	drizzly day
discover blue racer	in woods	bedtime
sketch plant specimens	in dining hall	second day
hear silly stories	in a national park	one night
observe raccoons	in cabin	fifth day

3. Describe the summer camp by discussing the various activities of the campers.

   _____

   _____

   _____

   _____

   _____

17

Another Place

Read the story. Complete the activity on page 19.

• •

Hello. My name is Ansal Khamba. I am twelve years old and attend a school in the city of Kolkata, India. My parents are both teachers. My father teaches Western literature in a college. If you are American, you might call this a "high school." My mother teaches world studies at the university. Both of my parents have gone to school in other countries as well as India. They have been to Cambridge, England; Cairo, Egypt; Boston, United States; and Bonn, Germany. They say I may go to school overseas if I want. But, I think I will stay in India. We have many good universities here.

My mother says I should tell you something about our country of Bharat. That is the official name of India. It would be difficult to tell you briefly about our country. It is very old and has at least 5,000 years of recorded history. Perhaps I will tell you about some of our beautiful sights instead.

My favorite place is the Taj Mahal. My parents took me there when I was seven years old. The towers of this magnificent structure rise high into the sky. An emperor named Shah Jahan ordered this building be created to honor his dead wife, Mumtaz Mahal. Twenty thousand workers worked twenty years to build this memorial, using white marble and red sandstone. They built reflecting pools and gardens outside.

When I was eight years old, my mother took me on a trip to the Bandhavgarh National Park. She said it was for my educational training. The many birds of the park are beautiful. I loved the blues and greens of the peacocks. The park is most famous for the care and protection it offers to tigers. It has more Bengal tigers than any other place in the world. The park is also home to lots of leopards too.

Two years ago, Father and Mother took me to the Thar Desert. What a harsh place! I cannot imagine anyone living in a land like that, yet many people do. They even hold desert festivals there every year. We traveled through the Thar Desert by safari, riding on camels.

This summer, we visited a region called Ladakh. There are many hills and mountains there. My family stayed in the home of a Tibetan family who were gracious hosts. After spending four days getting used to the high altitude, we hiked into the Zaskar Mountains. What a breathtaking view from so high up! We could look down across valleys of fields and villages. There are so many beautiful sights to see in my country!

Another Place (cont.)

1. How old is Ansal when he visits these places?

    a. Taj Mahal _____

    b. Thar Desert_____

    c. Bandhavgarh National Park_____

    d. Ladakh _____

2. Which place matches each thing?

    a. bird sanctuary_____

    b. magnificent structure _____

    c. large tiger population _____

    d. view from a mountain _____

    e. camel ride _____

3. Write a short description of one of the places in this story.

    _____

    _____

    _____

Name _____

Read the story. Write an answer to each question.

• •

Teddy almost fell out of his seat that Monday afternoon. Mrs. Beeker, his science teacher, announced to the class that they would soon be taking a trip. The following week, they would visit a nearby nature preserve to examine the wildlife in Dilly Pond! That meant Teddy would soon be able to see some leopard frogs!

In his area, leopard frogs could only be in Dilly Pond. Teddy had watched nature shows about them for years. This would finally be his chance to see them in person.

When the morning of September 25 arrived, the class boarded the bus in front of school. They rode off to the rural setting of Dilly Pond eighteen miles away. Students snapped pictures of crustaceans and small fish. They sketched pictures of plants along the pond. They observed birds, mammals, and amphibians in the wetlands community. Meanwhile, Teddy tiptoed through reeds, spying on dozens of fabulous frogs. He was in frog heaven!

That was thirty years ago, but Teddy still remembers. As he prepares the science laboratory for his students, his mind returns to that glorious afternoon so many years ago. It was the day that he first knew what he wanted to do with his life. It was one of the best days he could remember.

1. What three scenes are described in the story?

                      Time   Place

    a. _____   _____

    b. _____   _____

    c. _____   _____

2. What is Teddy's job today? _____

3. How did the class trip affect Teddy? _____

_____

Name _____

Listen, My Children

Read lines of dialogue from different stories. Match each set of quotes with a time and a place.

- -

Times	
on an autumn morning	late one afternoon
early spring	one summer night
on a wintry day	during baseball season

Places	
in a snowy field	in a big yard
on a beach	on a baseball field
in a living room	in a garden

1. Boom!
"Look, Dad! Don't those fireworks look pretty over the water? That last one looked like a dandelion."

Time: _____

_____

Place: _____

_____

2. "OK, do you have your rake?"
"I sure do. I can't wait to rake those leaves!"
"Well, I'm glad to have your help. As long as you don't jump into the piles when we're done."

Time: _____

_____

Place: _____

_____

3. "Wow! This is so much fun!"
"I know. Renting a snowmobile was a great idea."
"Can you ride toward those trees over there? Then, we'll stop and build a snowman."

Time: _____

_____

Place: _____

_____

4. "Ooh! See those flowers over there?"
"What are those called?"
"Well, the purple ones near that big maple are called lilacs."

Time: _____

_____

Place: _____

_____

5. "You're OUT!"
"What?"
"You're out of there!"
"Come on! That wasn't a strike."

Time: _____

_____

Place: _____

_____

Hemingway

Read the passage. Complete the activity on page 23. Circle the correct answers for the first two questions. Then, fill in a chart with descriptive words from the passage to describe Ernest Hemingway.

• •

Ernest Hemingway was one of the most influential writers of the twentieth century. His classic short stories and four major novels placed him in a class with other great American authors. Hemingway was a passionate person. He not only loved writing, but also outdoor adventure. He was also very driven and placed emotional and physical demands on himself and those around him. One of his sons once said that he "lived on a fast clock."

Hemingway was born in Oak Park, Illinois. After graduation from high school, he became a trainee at the Kansas City Star newspaper. It was there that he learned about writing and reporting. He once told a fellow writer, "Forget perfection. Keep [your characters as] people, people, people." He believed that no one was perfect. Everyone has good parts, but also bad parts. He followed that belief through all of his writing.

Hemingway tried to join the army at the age of 18. However, he was refused because he had poor vision. Instead, he became an ambulance driver and was sent to Italy during World War I. While serving on the front lines, he was wounded. He later received a medal for his bravery.

After the war, Hemingway moved to France. While living in Paris, he wrote a number of successful short stories. He also wrote *The Sun Also Rises,* a novel that became his first major success. Hemingway later moved to Key West, Florida where he worked on *A Farewell to Arms.* That novel was an instant success and helped him become famous all over the world.

During World War II, Hemingway worked as a reporter once again. When the war was over, he wrote the novel *The Old Man and the Sea.* It won him a Pulitzer Prize for fiction. Later in his life, he moved to Ketchum, Idaho, where he wrote his memoir. It was entitled *A Moveable Feast* and was his last great work.

Hemingway (cont.)

1. Which of these events happened first?

   a. He was wounded while driving an ambulance in Italy.

   b. He wrote the novel *A Farewell to Arms.*

   c. He attended school in Oak Park, Illinois.

   d. He became a reporter during World War II.

2. Which of these novels won Hemingway a Pulitzer Prize for fiction?

   a. *A Farewell to Arms*

   b. *The Old Man and the Sea*

   c. *The Sun Also Rises*

   d. *A Moveable Feast*

Ernest Hemingway

Name _____

Either, Or

A conflict is a problem in a story that a character must solve. Read the four stories. Write the two choices each character can make to solve his or her problem.

• •

1. Max had a difficult decision to make. He wanted to hang out with Tanya, but, she did not enjoy watching soccer. There was a big game scheduled for that afternoon, so, Max made plans to go to the game with Ted and Leon instead. Just as he hung up the phone, it rang again. It was Tanya. She was calling to see if he wanted to go with her to the new science fiction movie that had just opened. He had been dying to see it for weeks. What should he do?
    Either:_____
    Or: _____

2. Lee and Kip were arguing. Each boy believed that he deserved to claim the top prize at the science fair. They had both worked hard on their projects and each was sure that he would win. Jack was a friend to both Lee and Kip. He watched them dream up the ideas for their projects and put them together. So, they turned to him for his opinion. Which science project did he think was the best?
    Either:_____
    Or: _____

3. Mom gave me a choice. I could go with her and Dad to Aunt Terri's house. "You have not seen her in ages, and she is always asking when you are going to come for a visit," Mom had told me. Or, I could stay home and write letters to my relatives, inviting them to my end-of-school party. I really do not want to do either one on my weekend.
    Either:_____
    Or: _____

4. Janelle wanted to buy a gift for her twin sisters. Sabrina wanted a new baseball mitt. Yolanda wanted a dollhouse. She knew her sisters would enjoy those presents. But, she had also been thinking about buying them each a book. She wanted the twins to read more. Janelle could not afford the baseball mitt, the dollhouse, and the books. She was not sure what to do.
    Either:_____
    Or: _____

Name _____

Who Was Bessie Blount?

Read the passage. Write an answer to each question.

• •

Bessie Blount was an African American woman who lived in Virginia. She was born in 1914 during a difficult time for African Americans. At that time, black people and white people went to different schools.

As a result, Bessie did not have an easy childhood. She was also left-handed, which her teachers tried to discourage. Once, Bessie was punished for writing with her left hand. She decided to learn to write with either hand, as well as with her feet and even her teeth. Bessie was later forced out of school after she completed the sixth grade. However, she studied on her own and was able to go to college.

While in college, Blount studied physical therapy. She often worked with soldiers who had been injured in World War II. Many of them had lost the use of their arms and hands. She wanted to help them become independent. She taught them how to use their feet to do certain things.

Eating was the most difficult task many of her patients faced. They had trouble feeding themselves. To solve the problem, Blount invented a device that allowed her patients to eat independently. Manufacturers said it was too large and complicated, so, she was unable to sell it.

But, Blount did not give up. She decided to develop a simpler device instead. She created the "portable receptacle support." This was a brace that attached to a patient's neck. It could support a bowl, so a patient did not need hands to hold it.

Blount tried to sell the device to manufacturers and even to the Veterans Administration. Even though it was safe, simple, and effective, no one would buy it. In 1952, Blount signed over the rights to her feeding device to the French government. They wanted to use it in their military hospitals.

Even when she faced difficulties and rejection, Bessie Blount refused to give up. Today, she is remembered as an important inventor.

1. What were some challenges that Bessie Blount faced? _____

_____

_____

2. How did she overcome these challenges? _____

_____

_____

Name_____

Read the poem, which is in the form of a ballad. Complete the activity on page 27.

Refrain:
I sing a song to woo my love,
Far fairer than the stars above.
I will praise her name wherever I go,
While passing through this earth below.

(1)   We met by that old cherry tree.
       I glanced at her; she winked at me.
       I offered my pie, it was just a slice.
       I was sure she would think it was nice.

(2)   With pinky raised, she held her spoon.
       She scooped a bite that afternoon.
       Into her mouth this morsel traveled,
       And then she started to look baffled.

(3)   She gazed at me with watery eyes,
       And from her mouth there came a cry.
       She gagged; she turned and ran away.
       I have not seen her since that day.

(4)   I chased her but to no avail,
       Over hill and over dale.
       You see, I like my pie with spice.
       Chili powder tastes so nice!

(5)   There's more of this that I could tell;
       The movie rights for millions sell.
       Just sit beside me while I cry...
        Say, will you try a slice of pie?

A Balladeer's Tale (cont.)

1. What conflict does the balladeer have?_____

2. Why did his love run away? _____

3. When is this poem set—the past or present? _____

4. Is this poem written in first, second, or third person?_____

5. Who are the three characters?_____

6. Why might you not trust this balladeer? _____

7. What conflict or problem does the listener have at the end of the poem?
   _____

8. Does it seem like the speaker in the poem has learned anything from his problem? _____
   Why or why not? _____

9. The theme of a story or poem is the idea, viewpoint, or meaning that is found throughout the piece. The theme of the fairy tale "Cinderella," for example, could be stated as "good people triumph in the end."

Circle the best theme for "A Balladeer's Tale."

    human against Nature   good versus bad

          lost love   the value of friendship

Cracked Bell

Read the passage. Complete the activity on page 29.

• •

The Liberty Bell in Philadelphia is an important part of American history. It rang out from Independence Hall on July 8, 1776. The ringing bell was a signal, calling for the first public reading of the Declaration of Independence.

The bell had been commissioned by the Pennsylvania Assembly in 1751. They wanted to commemorate the golden anniversary of a charter. The charter was an important part of the city's history. It named rights and freedoms for the people of Pennsylvania. Words from the charter were etched into the face of the bell. They read, "Proclaim Liberty throughout all the land unto all the inhabitants thereof."

The bell was ordered from the city of London. It arrived in Philadelphia in September 1752. On the day that the bell was hung, it cracked during a test ring. The cause of the crack was probably a flaw in the bell.

Two workers named John Pass and John Stow were given the task of melting down the bell and recasting it. They added a bit more copper to make the bell less brittle. When the new bell was raised, people complained about its tone. The pair tried again, but people were unhappy with their next try as well.

Another bell was ordered from London. But when the new bell arrived, everyone was agreed that it did not sound any better. City leaders decided to keep the Pass and Stow bell. But, they would only ring it on special occasions.

The Pass and Stow bell rang out several times over the years. But, its most important ring was on July 8, 1776. It later became known as the Liberty Bell.

Eventually, the Liberty Bell cracked too. Exactly when it happened remains a mystery. But today, generations of Americans love the old bell for what it represents, crack and all.

Cracked Bell (cont.)

1. Why was the original bell ordered?

   a. to celebrate the anniversary of the new nation

   b. to announce the Declaration of Independence

   c. to commemorate the golden anniversary of a charter

   d. to call for freedom for Pennsylvania

2. Which of these events happened first?

   a. The Declaration of Independence was read in public.

   b. Pass and Stow recast the broken bell.

   c. The first bell arrived from London.

   d. A bell was commissioned by the Pennsylvania Assembly.

3. Which of these events happened last?

   a. City leaders did not like the sound of the new bell.

   b. The Liberty Bell also cracked.

   c. Pass and Stow melted down the broken bell.

   d. Pass and Stow raised their recreated bell.

4. What is the setting of the story in this passage?

   a. Philadelphia

   b. London

   c. New York

   d. Paris

5. When does the story in this passage take place?

   a. in the past

   b. in the present

   c. in the future

   d. time is unclear

29

Name _____

What Will Happen?

Read the start of two stories. Write an ending for each story.

• •

Neyla lived in a small house with a very small yard. She had always wanted a dog. So, she went to an animal shelter to pick one out. After looking at all of the dogs, she narrowed her choice down to two. The first was a large, black, one-year-old retriever. He had a lot of energy and was used to running on acres of land. The second dog was a small, three-year-old poodle. The people who had owned him said he stayed home alone all day and knew how to use a doggy door to go out to the yard.

1. What happens next?

    _____

    _____

    _____

Javon's weekend was very busy. Friday evening he had spent the evening at his friend Justin's house. They had stayed up late watching movies and playing cards. The next morning, he had to get up early for baseball practice. He was exhausted when he finally returned home, but he helped his mother get ready for the neighborhood party they were hosting that evening. When all of the preparations were finished, Javon decided to take a short nap.

2. What happens next?

    _____

    _____

    _____

Out of Order

Read seven stories. The events of each story are listed out of order below. Mark them from 1 to 4 to put them in the correct sequential order.

. . . .

A. _____ Now that she was awake, she was feeling thirsty.

_____ She headed toward the stream near the cave.

_____ It felt so good to lap up the cool, fresh water.

_____ Opening her eyes, the wild cat stretched.

B. _____ Armando threw on his clothes, then ran out to meet the school bus.

_____ Armando startled at the sound of the alarm clock and hit the snooze button.

_____ Half an hour later, he finally woke up.

_____ When the alarm sounded again, he slept through it.

C. _____ Moments later, a motorcade made its way down our street.

_____ The afternoon silence was broken by the sound of sirens.

_____ Police officers drove past, escorting a parade of shining vehicles.

_____ From the window of one car, I could see a world leader smiling and waving.

D. _____ Hal put some of the money in his secret hiding place and took the rest to the movies.

_____ "Sure thing, but be careful not to spend it all at once."

_____ "Dad, may I have my allowance early this week?"

_____ Hal ran to the living room to ask his dad for money.

E. _____ When I saw the price, I swallowed hard.

_____ My cousin whispered to me that it was a good deal.

_____ Now the baseball card was all mine!

_____ My hand shook as I handed over all that money.

F. _____ Instead of going toward the bowl, the hamster zipped under the bed.

_____ Sheri crawled on the floor with a flashlight, looking for her wayward pet.

_____ Sheri's hamster was curled up in her lap.

_____ She set the hamster on the ground, letting him waddle to his bowl.

G. _____ She searched the car for an umbrella with no success.

_____ Donna sighed when she reached the warm, dry shelter of the grocery store.

_____ Using an old newspaper to cover her head, she ran across the parking lot.

_____ Donna groaned as raindrops began to splat on the windshield.

Details, Details, Details

Read three stories. Describe the plot of each story. Then, list the most important details.

• •

1. Early one summer, a dragon arrived and began to roam all over the kingdom. Her strong wings flapped as she flew overhead shooting fireballs. She burned several farm fields and barns. There would be much less corn and potatoes to eat that winter. The king decided to set a curfew to keep the people safe. He hoped that the dragon would soon decide to leave.

Plot _____

_____

_____

Detail 1 _____

Detail 2 _____

Detail 3 _____

2. Today was a thrilling adventure from start to finish. A spider monkey ran off with my hat, and I could not get it back! But I did not care, because the monkey looked funny holding my baseball cap. We stopped to sketch the orchids, growing in brilliant colors from the trunks of the trees. While hiking up a steep trail, we heard a macaw screeching to its mate. I am so glad that Grandma and Grandpa brought me to Costa Rica for vacation.

Plot _____

_____

_____

Detail 1 _____

Detail 2 _____

Detail 3 _____

Current Events

Read newspaper articles based on three stories. Write your own title for each one.

• •

1. Kansas: A young girl, injured during the area's recent tornado, regained consciousness on Saturday. However, her aunt reports that the child remains confused and claims that she recently visited a land called Oz. "Clearly, my niece requires more rest and possibly further medical treatment," stated the aunt. "I mean, she's talking about flying monkeys and all sorts of shenanigans."

Title _____

2. Martha's Vineyard: Mr. Sylvester "Sly" Fox went on a long hike yesterday. He returned home, exhausted and dehydrated. When asked why he attempted the hike without supplies, Mr. Fox answered that he expected to be able to eat the wild grapes that grow throughout the area. However, the only cluster of grapes he could find dangled well out of his reach. He tried and tried to reach the grapes, but had no success.

Title _____

3. Charming Palace: The royal family has announced the engagement of Prince Charming, to a Miss C. Ella. The engagement followed swiftly after the couple' s first meeting at a ball held last week on the palace grounds. According to ball attendees, Miss Ella dramatically disappeared from the ball at the stroke of midnight. The prince demanded a search of the entire region. The search party had only a single dancing shoe with which to identify the missing woman. When she was located, witnesses say the prince promptly proposed.

Title _____

The Gathering

Read the story. List the main events from the story in the correct order. Three events have already been filled in for you.

• •

Molly and her dad, Mike, were on their way to Uncle Don's house. Uncle Don had invited all the family together to welcome back Molly and her father. The two had lived in Cades Center, but moved across the country when Mike got his teaching job at Welliston College. This was their first time back in three years.

The house was brightly lit.

As Mike maneuvered their old Mustang down Uncle Don's street, he noticed the house was brightly lit. There were plenty of cars out front. The garage door was wide open, so people could enter the house through the attached garage. That was just like Uncle Don!

Molly and her father knocked, but no one came to greet them. But, the front door was open, so they decided to go in. They yelled hello, but no one seemed to hear. That is when they heard party noises coming up from the basement. Aha! The family must be downstairs!

Molly had brought a layer cake for the gathering, but she needed a knife to serve it. She also needed forks to go with the paper plates she had brought. So, she stopped in the kitchen to search for the utensils. While she was in the kitchen, Mike walked to the stairway and headed down to the party.

Molly felt bewildered. Sure, it had been three years since she had been in the house, but the kitchen looked so different. She was almost positive that the sink had been under the window. The new cabinets seemed too modern for Uncle Don's taste, and whose pictures were on the refrigerator door?

Meanwhile, Mike rushed down to the basement with excitement. He could not wait to see all of his family again. When he came to the bottom of the steps, he greeted the women there with a hearty hello. It was odd that he did not know any of them, though. They must be friends from Uncle Don's business, he thought.

Mike went into the next room where he found four people playing cards. They warmly greeted him, and he heartily shook hands with everyone. Then, he grabbed a handful of chips and opened a can of soda.

Mike scanned their faces.

The Gathering (cont.)

But as he munched on his chips, panic began to set in as Mike entered a third room and looked around. Eight or nine adults sat watching an action film playing on TV. Mike scanned their faces.

Quickly, Mike spun about and raced up the stairs. Halfway up, he met Molly, who was just on her way down with the cake, plates, and forks in hand. "Quick, we need to turn around," Mike called.

Molly was confused, but followed her father without question. As they re-entered the kitchen Mike said, "We're in the wrong house, honey. Let's get out of here now!"

Quick, we need to turn around.

They dropped off the utensils, dashed back outside to the car, started it up, and fled down the street. About half a block down, they came to another familiar-looking house with cars, lights, and music galore. It was Uncle Don's; this time they had the right house. Embarrassed, the two headed into the house with the cake.

Uncle Don greeted them at the door with a phone in hand, wearing a smile. "Well, well, well, decided to do some breaking and entering on your way over?" he asked them.

Molly and Mike froze with fear, but Uncle Don burst out laughing. "I am only kidding. My neighbor figured you two had gotten confused. He called to tell me you had a slight detour but would be arriving soon. We're all invited to join his party later. Welcome home!"

1. _____
2. _____
3. Molly is puzzled as she searches for the knife.
4. _____
5. _____
6. _____
7. Mike gazes at the people in the television room.
8. _____
9. _____
10. Mike and Molly drive down the street.
11. _____
12. _____

The Best Bunny

Read the story. Complete the activity on page 37.

• •

It had all started two weeks before spring break. Spring made Marcus think of chicks, ducklings, and cute baby rabbits. Oh, how Marcus wanted a rabbit! He made the mistake of sharing this wish at the breakfast table. Mom raised her eyebrow, his older brother Al questioned where they would keep a rabbit in their apartment, and his baby sister Lori nearly choked on her cornflakes.

Marcus shut his mouth, deciding to keep his wishes to himself. Of course, there was no way he could have a rabbit. It just was not possible.

Marcus tried not to think about the rabbit and stayed busy instead. He played baseball with his friends, rearranged the books, models, and building sets on the shelves in his room, rescued a pile of dirty clothes that had been under his bed since last winter, and reread three comic books.

But, no matter how much he tried to distract himself, Marcus could not keep his mind off of his wish. He still wanted a rabbit. On the last day of spring break, Marcus resigned himself to the fact that he would not be getting a rabbit. He decided to get his clothes together for school the next day. He trudged to the kitchen, where his mother was baking sweet rolls. Al was on the phone, planning an outing with some of his high school friends.

"Mom, do you know where my new blue shirt is?" Marcus asked. "Oh. I took it out of the dryer, and it's hanging in the laundry room."

Marcus walked down the hall. The laundry room was really a catch-all: it had a pantry, a storage closet, and of course a washing machine and dryer. Marcus pulled on the door handle, but the door was locked. That was strange because that door was never locked!

"Hey, Mom! Why is this door locked?"

"What?" called Mom, wiping flour and dough from her hands with a dish towel. "The door's locked? We don't lock this door." Marcus heard a sound behind the door. It was not loud, hardly a thump or thud, and was more like the scratch of a fingernail on tiled floor.

Mom took down a key from over the door frame, slid it into the lock, and opened the door.

The door was never locked!

The Best Bunny (cont.)

Put events from the story in the correct order. Write first, second, third, and so on.

• •

There on the floor was one small, lop-eared rabbit, with pink eyes and white-fur. Lori sat on the floor beside the bunny with a big grin on her face. "Surprise!" she sang out as Al joined them in the laundry room.

" We have got a cage for the rabbit in the building garage, but we should buy some feed for him soon," his mother told him.

As Marcus sat down on the floor, Lori handed him a white, furry ball. "Al and I picked him up yesterday. Isn't he cute?" she said. His new rabbit was not just cute, Marcus thought. It was the best bunny in the world.

His family understood.

Marcus held his rabbit, too shocked to say a word. But, his family understood, and they were pleased that he was so happy.

1. _____ Marcus decides to get his clothes ready for school.

2. _____ Marcus read old comic books.

3. _____ His mother unlocks the laundry room door.

4. _____ Marcus played baseball with friends.

5. _____ Mom was baking sweet rolls in the kitchen.

6. _____ Al and Lori react badly to Marcus's idea of having a rabbit.

7. _____ Marcus tells his family that he would like a rabbit.

8. _____ Marcus heard a scratching noise from the laundry room.

9. _____ Marcus was too moved to say a word.

10. _____ A lop-eared rabbit was on the floor of the laundry room.

11. _____ Marcus decided to keep his wishes to himself.

Name _____

Person to Person

Below are nine short paragraphs. Identify the point of view for each one. Write "first person" if the narrator uses "I" or "we." Write "second person" if the narrator uses "you." Write "third person" if the narrator uses "he," "she," or "they."

• •

_____ A. You are on a deserted island: no town, no people; just you and those crazy, noisy seagulls. What are you going to do?

_____ B. She fled toward the castle to beg the gatekeeper for entrance. Running at a breakneck pace, she sped toward the tall, wooden gate.

_____ C. Maggie bit her lip. No use crying about it. She pulled her math homework out of the sink and just stared at her little sister.

_____ D. Yesterday was not the best day at our house. The dog ate all the cereal, so we had nothing for breakfast but orange juice. I was in the middle of my shower when the hot water heater went out, and the shower turned freezing cold. Worst of all, my bike had a flat tire, so I had to walk all the way to school.

_____ E. You have too many important things to plan. Who should you invite to the party? What should you serve your guests? And on, and on.

_____ F. I was so proud of myself. I had studied and studied for that test. All that hard work was worth it because I got an A.

_____ G. When he woke up this morning, Tom looked out the open window and breathed deeply. The air was fresh and cool and made him alive with anticipation. Today was the big game!

_____ H. Columbus stood on the deck of the ship. He could clearly see land on the horizon. Land! He was sure that he would make his fortune there.

_____ I. The sky is clear. Not too much of a breeze. The weather is perfect. That is why your heart is thumping, you know. It is time to do it once and for all. You have got to jump out of the plane and prove that you can skydive.

Name _____

First, Second, or Third?

Below are nine short paragraphs. Identify the point of view for each one. Write "first person" if the narrator uses "I" or "we." Write "second person" if the narrator uses "you." Write "third person" if the narrator uses "he," "she," or "they."

• •

_____ A. It's true, you know? You always loved cats more than people. When you first saw . . . what was that cat's name? Oh, yes, Bernard! When your dad brought Bernard home from the shelter, you looked like you had gone to heaven and seen an angel.

_____ B. Turkeys are strange birds. They have long necks with floppy waddles. Their back feathers spread out like a fan. They make strange gobbling noises and do not even fly. Plus, they have the same name as the country turkey. What a weird animal!

_____ C. Mama said that if I was a good girl, I could get a balloon. So, I did not fuss in the grocery store. I did not whine at the dry cleaners. I did not even pout at the post office. Finally, when we finished all of the errands, I got my prize—a bright, red balloon!

_____ D. Patches McCloud had better move out of his termite-infested apartment before the walls come tumbling in on him! This is the last warning!

_____ E. When you were born, the sun smiled down upon the earth. The moon glowed. The creatures of the night forest whispered that you, a princess, had been born.

_____ F. She carried a large basket of laundry on her head. She had done chores like this since she was a tiny child. But, this time things were different. Mikaela was working at a real job now. Her mother would be so proud!

_____ G. Oh, it was so dark! We will never know what caused the sudden blackout at the ball game. We hope the game will be rescheduled.

_____ H. The song "Yankee Doodle" was used by British soldiers to mock the colonials who opposed them. But, the colonists were smart enough to realize that if they embraced the mockery, it would take the sting out of it. The song became their anthem!

_____ I. It is backbreaking work. All day long, we bend over at the waist as we carefully replant our rice in the flooded paddy. But, our feet tingle in the cool, rich, oozing mud.

Name_____

Read the poem. Write answers to the first three questions. Circle the correct answers for the last two questions.

• •

A rabbit once went to a pond
To drink the water, clear and cool,
It spied a fish with silver scales,
Glide gently across the pool.

"You are beautiful," the rabbit said.
"Look how you dive and soar!
I want to be your friend, dear Fish,
Come play upon the shore."

"The sun is warm, the grass is soft.
Sweet berries fall from bush and tree,
We can leap and jump and thump,
In morning air, so cool and free."

"You are a friendly rabbit,"
The fish replied with a smile.
I wish that I could come on shore.
And laugh and play awhile.

"But I cannot come on land,
The sun would burn my scales, you see.
I need water to breathe, not air
And berries taste weird to me."

"I live in water; you live on land.
We are different it is true.
But, if you visit from time to time,
I will be a fun friend for you!"

1. Who are the two speakers in this poem?

    a. _____

    b. _____

2. Explain the story of the poem.

    _____

    _____

3. What do you think the theme of this poem is? Write it in one phrase or sentence.

    _____

    _____

4. Circle two adjectives to describe the first speaker in the poem:

    hopeful   angry   sad   excited   silly

5. Circle two adjectives to describe the second speaker in the poem:

    annoyed   bitter   practical   exhilarated   wistful

Name _____

What is What?

Each sentence below has a specific purpose. If it relates to character traits, write C. If it adds to the plot of a story, write P. If it identifies a setting, write S.

• •

_____ 1. It was a dark and stormy night.

_____ 2. Uncle Matt was as forgetful as ever.

_____ 3. She danced for hours, never knowing about the gift given to her by the green-clad elves.

_____ 4. Dina could not stand her older brother's constant teasing.

_____ 5. During the night, the clouds lifted, and the moon rose brilliantly against the dark sky.

_____ 6. They enjoyed gliding along the smooth surface of the lake, just outside the old log cabin.

_____ 7. As Daisy darted after the butterfly, I tried to follow the dog, but soon lost my way.

_____ 8. Ike knocked on the door three times, but when no one came to the entrance, he turned away dejectedly.

_____ 9. The emperor's courtyard was filled with snow-white swans.

_____ 10. Mother's favorite thing was telling stories about her childhood.

_____ 11. Jerry met his sister to shop for their grandmother's present.

_____ 12. At the top of the hill was a flat, open plain with only a few gray-green boulders breaking the grassy surface.

_____ 13. Henry wandered into the forest to look for his lost cow.

_____ 14. It all started on the morning the sixth-graders climbed onto the bus for a class trip to the museum.

_____ 15. It was no secret that Rob hated doing chores more than doing anything else.

_____ 16. Goldilocks ran from the bears' cottage and was never seen again.

_____ 17. Fido often disobeyed, but was such a friendly dog that no one seemed to care.

Who, What, Where?

Answer the questions for the following three paragraphs.

• •

1. Henry stepped out of the car and lifted its hood. Muttering under his breath, he checked the hoses and the radiator for leaks. Steam rose in thick puffs of hot, wet gas. Henry walked to the passenger's window. "Sorry, Sara," he said. "I am afraid we're stuck here until help arrives. The radiator is low on water."

    Who are the characters? _____

    What is the conflict? _____

    What is the setting? _____

2. Dana hobbled over to the bench at the end of the third quarter. When she went for the rebound a couple of minutes ago, Number 43 had clobbered her! The fall was embarrassing enough, but she twisted her ankle too! She just had to stay in the game; it meant everything to her. Looking up, she saw that Coach wanted her in the huddle. Good, Dana thought. He had not noticed! She caught her breath at the pain as she stood. Uh oh, it seemed that Dana could not put any pressure on her ankle right now.

    Who are the characters? _____

    What is the conflict? _____

    What is the setting? _____

3. The whole class had gone cross-country skiing. We were supposed to stick together, however I lost my group of ten skiers. I figured I could catch up with them by following their tracks. But, I figured wrong! There were all sorts of trails made by skiers from at least ten different schools. Plus, an inch of falling snow added to my confusion. There I was in the middle of a snowy scene with no familiar faces in sight.

    Who are the characters? _____

    What is the conflict? _____

    What is the setting? _____

Name _____

The Perfect Place

Match each genre with its most appropriate setting.

. . . .

_____ 1. in the star system of a distant planet

_____ 2. on the balcony of a prince's castle

_____ 3. in the den of a crafty fox

_____ 4. in a land beyond the mountains

_____ 5. in the office of a private detective

_____ 6. alone in the forest with only a pocketknife, a magnifier, and a good pair of hiking boots

_____ 7. at a ranch out on the frontier

_____ 8. at the edge of the Brazilian rainforest filled with wildlife

_____ 9. on a busy college campus

    a. a mystery

    b. a romance

    c. a realistic story

    d. a science fiction story

    e. a western

    f. an environmental documentary

    g. a folktale

    h. a survival story

    i. an animal story

10. Choose one of the settings above and describe it in 3–5 sentences.

_____

_____

_____

_____

Name _____

 Go, Man, Go!

Read the story. Complete the activity on page 45 by filling in each web using details from the story. Then, answer the questions.

• •

They stretched in midfield, preparing for the morning's events. Theo, dressed in the red and white of his school, prepared alongside the rest of the seventeen athletes who had come to the meet from Weston Middle School.

Theo was hardworking, and he had trained well. Now, on this warm and bright May morning, it was time to prove his worth, and Theo found he was very nervous. Twenty-two schools were participating in the invitational meet. The field was filled with athletes dressed in their brightly colored jerseys. Weston's girls had already scored points in the long jump and javelin. The boys had done well too. They placed second and fourth in the pole vault. Not bad, considering that track and field was a brand-new sport to Weston Middle School.

Theo's main event was the 400-meter dash. It was what he dreamed of running ever since he saw his Uncle Dave's victorious sprint seven years ago. Yet, these meets made Theo so nervous. As he shook off the jitters, Theo saw a lone figure at the long jump pit. He was a thin boy roughly Theo's height and build. He wore the only gray shirt in the wild mass of school colors.

Even though he looked out of place, the boy seemed calm and sure of himself. Theo introduced himself to the runner, a friendly, determined student named Carl Alvarez. Carl was the only athlete from his school. He had taken two city buses to get there, and he was just there for the 400-meter race. Like Theo, this was his first year in track and field. Carl did not seem fazed to be alone, though; he told Theo he wanted to start a team at his school. Returning to his own team, Theo admitted to himself that Carl's attitude was impressive.

When the 400 was announced and Theo lined up, the Weston team started to chant. They were getting pumped up for the race. Theo glanced at Carl, who did not have anyone to cheer for him, but Carl seemed focused and ready for his race. As the pistol fired, the race began. The crowded field of runners—sixteen boys in eight lanes—sprinted down the stretch. The Weston team yelled, "Go, man, go!" Every Weston student screamed as Theo took the lead coming out of the first curve.

Theo's heart pounded as he crossed over to the inside lane. He was ahead of the others! Footsteps thudded behind him as he entered the wide, final turn. Someone was pulling alongside him. It was Carl! Around the curve he ran, Carl at his side matching him step for step, yet never falling back. The two boys sped into the final stretch. Theo raced as never before, neck to neck with his challenger. He wondered who would take the prize.

© Carson-Dellosa   **44**   Story Elements • CD-104558

Go, Man, Go! (cont.)

Theo   **Carl**

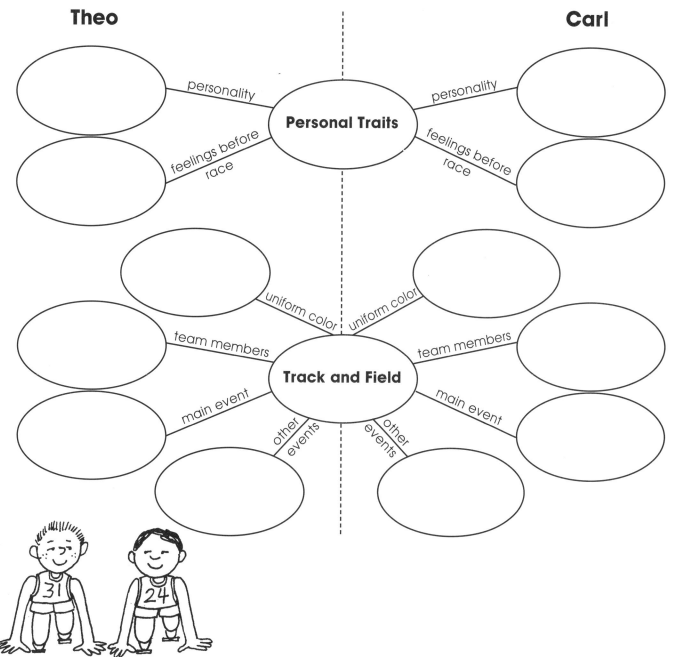

1. How many schools were at the meet? _____
2. What created so much color on the field? _____
3. How long had Theo been training? _____
4. In what month does this story take place? _____
5. Describe the weather on the day of the meet. _____
6. Who do you think won the race? _____

45

Answer Key

Page 4
Circle: 1. science fiction; 2. poetry;
3. historical fiction; 4. biography;
5. folktale; Write: 6. fairy tale;
7. science fiction; 8. biography;
9. fantasy; 10. poetry

Page 5
Circle: 1. science fiction; 2. fantasy;
3. historical fiction; 4. realistic fiction

Page 6
1. biography; 2. tall tale; 3. science
fiction; 4. realistic fiction; 5. myth;
6. tall tale

Page 7
1. f; 2. d; 3. b; 4. a; 5. c; 6. e; 7. i; 8. h;
9. j; 10. k; 11. l; 12. g; 13.–18. Answers
will vary.

Page 8
1. R; 2. R; 3. F; 4. R; 5. R; 6. F; 7. F; 8. R;
9. R; 10. F

Page 9
1. b; 2. e; 3. i; 4. a; 5. f; 6. h; 7. d; 8. j;
9. c; 10. g

Pages 10–11
Place an X: 1. c; 2. a; 3. a; 4. b

Page 12
1. g; 2. a; 3. d; 4. c; 5. h; 6. b; 7. e; 8. f

Page 13
1. a boy's bedroom; 2. Cal and
Cleo, twin brother and sister; 3. They
need enough money to go to an
amusement park. 4. They decide to
rake their neighbors' leaves for cash.

Page 14
1. Ned Tuttle, 2. Dorothy Wells;
3. Lonnie Lorenzo; 4. Helene; 5. Dora
the deer mouse; 6. Lady Beatrice;
7. Steven

Page 15
1. b; 2. d; 3. e; 4. a; 5. c; 6.–10.
Answers will vary.

Pages 16–17
1. summer; camp; 2. see baby
possums/in crook of the beech tree/
second day; sing songs/in dining
hall/every noon; discover blue
racer/in field/fifth day; sketch plant
specimens/in a national park/a
drizzly day; hear silly stories/in cabin/
bedtime; observe raccoons/in
woods/one night; 3. Answers will vary;
campers live in cabins; they visit a
national park for nature hikes; there is
a lake and a large dining hall, etc.

Pages 18–19
1. a. 7; b. 10; c. 8; d. 12; 2.
a. Bandhavgarh; b. Ladakh;
c. Bandhavgarh; d. Ladakh; e. Thar
Desert; 3. Answers will vary.

Page 20

I. a. Monday afternoon; school;
b. September 25; Dilly Pond; c. Thirty
years later; school; 2. He is a science
teacher. 3. It helped him know what
he wanted to do with his life.

Page 21

I. one summer night; on a beach;
2. on an autumn morning; in a big
yard; 3. on a wintry day; in a snowy
field; 4. early spring; in a garden;
5. during baseball season; on a
baseball field

Pages 22–23

Circle: I. c; 2. b; Fill in: influential,
passionate, driven, famous

Page 24

I. go to the game; go to the movie;
2. agree with Kip; agree with Lee;
3. go to aunt's; write to relatives;
4. buy the toys the twins want; buy
books for them

Page 25

I. Answers may vary. She was African
American; she was a woman; she
was left-handed; she was forced
to quit school after sixth grade;
manufacturers in the U.S. would not
buy her inventions. 2. She learned to
write with both hands, her feet, and
her teeth; she studied on her own;
she took her inventions to Europe; she
worked hard; she never quit trying.

Pages 26–27

I. His love has run away. 2. She ran
away because he put chili powder
in a pie. 3. the present; 4. first person;
5. the speaker, the lost love, and the
listener to the balladeer's tale;
6. because he puts strange spices
in his pies; 7. whether or not to refuse
a piece of pie; 8. No; he lost his love
over his pie recipe, but there is no
evidence that he has changed his
recipe. 9. lost love

Pages 28–29

Circle: I. c; 2. d; 3. b; 4. a; 5. a

Page 30

Answers will vary.

Page 31

A. 2, 3, 4, I; B. 4, I, 3, 2; C. 2, I, 3, 4;
D. 4, 3, 2, I; E. I, 2, 4, 3; F. 3, 4, I, 2;
G. 2, 4, 3, I

Page 32

I. Plot: A dragon was roaming
through a kingdom. Detail I: Farms
and barns were burned. Detail 2: The
king set a curfew. Detail 3: He hoped
the dragon would decide to leave.
2. Plot: The narrator is on vacation in
Costa Rica. Detail I: Spider monkey
takes the narrator's hat. Detail 2: The
narrator sketches flowers. Detail 3:
The narrator hikes up steep trail and
hears a macaw.

Page 33

Answers will vary.

Pages 34–35

1. Mike and Molly drive to Uncle Don's house. 2. They let themselves into the house. 3. Molly is puzzled as she looks for the knife. 4. Molly notices that the kitchen is different. 5. Mike enters the party. 6. Mike enters the card room. 7. Mike gazes at the people in the television room. 8. Mike races up stairs. 9. Mike tells Molly they are leaving. 10. Mike and Molly drive down the street. 11. Mike and Molly arrive at the right house. 12. They are all invited to the neighbor's party.

Pages 36–37

1. sixth; 2. fifth; 3. ninth; 4. fourth; 5. seventh; 6. second; 7. first; 8. eighth; 9. eleventh; 10. tenth; 11. third

Page 38

A. second person; B. third person; C. third person; D. first person; E. second person; F. first person; G. third person; H. third person; I. second person

Page 39

A. second person; B. third person; C. first person; D. third person; E. second person; F. third person; G. first person; H. third person; I. first person

Page 40

1. a. a rabbit; b. a fish, 2. A rabbit wants the fish to come on land to play. The fish explains it is impossible, but they can still be friends.

3. Answers will vary; one possible answer is "Differences do not need to interfere with friendship." 4. hopeful; excited; 5. wistful; practical

Page 41

1. S; 2. C; 3. P; 4. C; 5. S; 6. S; 7. P; 8. P; 9. S; 10. C; 11. P; 12. S; 13. P; 14. P; 15. C; 16. P; 17. C

Page 42

1. Henry, Sara; they need water for their radiator; along a road; 2. Dana, Coach, Player Number 43; Dana's ankle is hurt. basketball court during a game; 3. first-person narrator, group of skiers from different schools; the narrator is lost; the woods in wintertime.

Page 43

1. d; 2. b; 3. i; 4. g; 5. a; 6. h; 7. e; 8. f; 9. c; 10. Answers will vary.

Pages 44–45

Web answers for Theo: personality: hardworking, disciplined; feelings before race: nervous; uniform color: red and white; team members: seventeen; main event: 400-meter dash; other events: high jump; Web answers for Carl: personality: friendly, determined; feelings before race: calm; uniform color: none (gray t-shirt); team members: no team; main event: 400-meter dash; other events: none; 1. 22; 2. uniforms from all the schools; 3. since early March (3 months); 4. May; 5. warm, sunny; 6. Answers will vary.

Story Elements • CD-104558